Investing

Strategies For Accumulating Riches And Attaining
Economic Independence Through A Broadened
Investment Portfolio Utilizing Index Funds

*(The Definitive Manual For Generating Income On Fiverr
And Unveiling Success Strategies For Clickbank)*

Anastacio Juan

TABLE OF CONTENT

Currency. Alternate Formulation: "Subsequent To That, Additional Forms Of Digital Currencies Have Come Into Existence."

The cryptographic nature of cryptocurrency units is the sole means by which ownership can be verified.

Alternative cryptocurrencies or altcoins encompass tokens, digital currencies, and various forms of digital assets that are distinct from bitcoin.

Alternative cryptocurrencies often exhibit underlying differences from bitcoin. Ethereum boasts the highest level of blockchain adoption on a global scale and possesses the most substantial following among alternative cryptocurrencies.

A blockchain is an ever-evolving register of records, known as blocks, which are interconnected and secured through the implementation of cryptography.

According to the design, blockchains are resistant to any modifications of the data. A blockchain provides an authoritative record of the ownership and validity of every digital currency's tokens. The vast majority of digital currencies aim to gradually reduce the issuance of that currency, establishing a maximum limit on the overall quantity of that money that will ever be in circulation.

The digital currency held within a wallet is not tied to individuals, but instead to one or more specific cryptographic keys.

The identities of Bitcoin owners remain anonymous, although all transactions are publicly accessible on the blockchain.

Cryptocurrencies are primarily employed outside the realm of established financial institutions and regulatory bodies, and are exchanged electronically over the internet.

Cryptocurrency transactions facilitate the exchange of digital assets, enabling clients to trade cryptocurrencies for various resources, including conventional fiat currencies, or conduct conversions between different digital currencies.

There is currently a utilization of ATMs for cryptocurrencies with ongoing development of additional units. You have the option to employ a card, such as a charge/Visa, in order to withdraw funds and make payments for your purchases (although this may not be widely accessible at present).

Cryptocurrency networks exhibit a lack of regulation that has been criticized for enabling criminal entities to evade taxes and engage in money laundering.

Transactions conducted via the utilization and exchange of these alternative cryptocurrencies operate independently from established financial frameworks, thereby facilitating potential tax evasion.

Several of the leading Cryptocurrencies include:

- Bitcoin. The most known crypto. Initially conceived and implemented in the year 2008, and has been actively employed since the following year.

- Ethereum. Otherwise called ETH. It possesses a decentralized programming platform that enables the creation and execution of applications. The primary aim of Ethereum is to establish a decentralized framework for financial products that can be accessed by individuals worldwide, regardless of their personal identity, nationality, or religious beliefs. Ethereum is a developmental phase that leverages blockchain technology, allowing individuals to engage in transactions using a cryptocurrency known as ether. Currently, it holds the position of the second-largest digital currency, following Bitcoin.

• Litecoin. Otherwise called LTC. It boasts a faster rate of blockage compared to Bitcoin, consequently resulting in expedited confirmation times for transactions. There is a growing contingent of merchants who accept Litecoin.

• Cardano. Otherwise called ADA. Currently in its nascent stages. Its aim is to establish a decentralized financial ecosystem with the goal of becoming the global monetary infrastructure.

• Bitcoin Cash. Otherwise called BCH. It demonstrates a greater capacity for expeditious transaction processing compared to the Bitcoin network. Delays in proceedings are more constrained and associated expenses are reduced.

• Stellar. Additionally, know and XLM. Designed to facilitate communication between financial institutions for large-scale transactions. Significant transactions between banks and venture companies, which typically necessitate several days and substantial financial resources, can now be executed almost instantaneously and with minimal costs, eliminating the need for intermediaries. It remains an accessible blockchain that is open for utilization by all. The framework accounts for cross-border transactions involving various currencies. The organization anticipates that clients will possess Lumens in order to carry out transactions on the network.

• Binance Coin. Otherwise called BNB. It represents a platform where clients can engage in the trading of digital coins and utilize BNB to convert various cryptocurrencies from one form to another.

• Tether. Otherwise called USDT. A crucial aspect of the aggregation of stable coins entails tethering their value to a currency or some external benchmark in order to mitigate volatility.

• Our aim is to reduce price differences in order to attract potential customers who may otherwise be hesitant. The cost of ties is directly linked to the value of the US dollar.

- Monero. Otherwise called XMR. This currency offers a high level of security, confidentiality, and anonymity.

Conduct thorough research before incorporating cryptocurrencies into your investment portfolio. Cryptos are risky.

Investing in digital forms of currency entails a notable degree of speculation. This market exhibits a remarkably volatile nature, thereby posing a tangible risk of substantial financial losses.

Advantages of cryptos:

- Cryptocurrencies provide fast and cost-effective money transfers. This factor contributes to the widespread popularity of using them for international money transfers.

• Cryptocurrencies are not subject to control by authorities and cannot be subjected to freezing.

• There is a prevailing belief held by certain individuals that they represent the currency of the future.

• Certain allies appreciate the ability of digital currency to obviate the involvement of national banks in the management of the currency supply, as these banks have been known to have certain issues over time.

decrease the value of currency through the process of inflation

• Cryptocurrencies possess global reach, engendering uniform valuation across nations.

• Cryptocurrencies are transacted peer-to-peer online, eliminating the need for intermediaries.

• Bitcoin exchanges maintain a high level of confidentiality and anonymity.

• Minimal, insignificant charges

• Fast

• Non-inflationary

• Payment freedom

• The authority to revoke it cannot be exercised by central legislatures.

Disadvantages of cryptos:

• The ultimate outcome of cryptocurrency is not guaranteed. Investors seeking to make predictions in this market are advised to adhere to the most widely recognized cryptocurrencies such as bitcoin, ethereum, and litecoin.

• As digital currencies lack a central repository and exist solely in virtual form, it is possible for a ledger balance to be depleted. In the event that a client misplaces the private key to their wallet, the digital currency under their ownership becomes irretrievable.

• Fraudsters can also hijack an individual's mobile account through impersonation of an account holder.

• Very speculative

• A considerable number of individuals still lack awareness regarding cryptocurrencies.

• Potential government interference. • The likelihood of governmental obstruction. • The prospect of obstruction from the government. • The chance of government hindrance. • The risk of government thwarting. They can be banned.

• Absence of legal remedies

• Employed in illicit tax evasion/unregulated market transactions

In order to acquire digital currencies, it is imperative to possess a wallet, an online application designed to securely store your currency.

Upon documenting a transaction, one may subsequently initiate the transfer of actual funds in order to acquire cryptocurrencies.

Exclusively employ a wallet issued by a reputable establishment. Do your research. Coinbase and Binance are globally renowned platforms for facilitating the trading of bitcoin, with a significant market presence.

If you have a requirement to acquire bitcoin and other cryptocurrencies and subsequently sell them,

Several fees to consider include transaction costs, deposit fees, withdrawal fees, and trading fees.

"Chapter III: The Process of Purchasing a Personal Residence

Having homeownership serves as a fundamental pillar of prosperity, encompassing not only financial opulence but also providing a sense of emotional stability.

– Suze Orman, a renowned financial advisor, author, and host of online webcasts

Why allocate resources towards real estate if you do not possess your own dwelling? This represents the inception of embarking on a journey to become a real estate investor. In addition to serving as an excellent source of capital for your investment endeavors and a desirable domicile for your family, your property will also contribute to safeguarding a portion of your hard-earned income. The revenue and expenses associated with your home loan can be organized and, with a few exceptions, deducted from your earned income.

Besides investment funds, a mortgage or equity loan represents the most economical means of financing the purchase of investment properties.

Acquiring a perpetual abode for personal utilization entails, and rightly so, a notably more emotive journey compared to the pursuit of an investment property. Undoubtedly, sentiment should never play a role when acquiring investment property!

The optimal approach for both yourself and your family is to select a locality or town, and subsequently endeavor to acquire a advantageous arrangement within that vicinity. I will guide you systematically through some of the crucial decisions you must undertake when purchasing your initial residence. Irrespective of your current home ownership status, a substantial portion of the information detailed in this section will be applicable when acquiring investment properties.

Meeting the Eligibility Criteria for a Mortgage Loan

There is absolutely no valid rationale for contemplating properties that are beyond one's financial means. Consequently, prior to embarking on a house search, it is imperative to have a comprehensive understanding of the extent to which you would be eligible for a mortgage loan. This will constitute a determinant of your compensation, your FICO score, and your present financial obligations.

Generally, banks will allow a maximum debt-to-income ratio of 44%, considering the entirety of your outstanding debts relative to your net income.

This signifies that if your monthly salary amounts to $5,000, you can allocate a maximum of 44% or $2,200 each month towards debt. This encompasses expenses such as mortgage payments, car loans, student loans, credit card bills, and any other forms of revolving credit recorded on your credit report.

This excludes expenditures related to electricity, telecommunication services, water consumption, as well as costs incurred for food and any other discretionary expenses.

Engaging in substantial financial commitments, such as vehicle installments or other substantial monthly expenses, can substantially limit the affordability of the home you can acquire. Please bear this in mind when making purchases with a credit card. In addition to adversely impacting your credit score, it also impairs your borrowing capabilities. The bank or a qualified professional will perform the necessary calculations on your behalf and inform you about the highest monthly payment you can adopt, and therefore the most expensive property within your affordability.

After obtaining a mortgage, the monthly installment for your home loan will vary depending on factors such as the duration of amortization, the interest rate, and the amount financed.

Amortization refers to the duration required to settle your loan. It is possible for you to acquire a credit with a balloon payment due in seven years (or alternative duration), yet it will be amortized over a period exceeding 30 years.

Amortization tables can be conveniently accessed on various websites, such as BankRate.com.

By entering the numerical values, the table yields the corresponding result. Allocate some effort towards acquainting yourself with the amortization table, as it will play a significant role in your transactions.

integral aspect of your investments. If you become aware of the prevailing market interest rate, you will be able to expeditiously ascertain the corresponding payment for a residence of any value.

For example, let us consider a scenario where the intention is to acquire a permanent residence for a total cost of $212,000, utilizing a loan-to-value ratio of 100%. The interest rate on the loan is 3.25%, and the repayment period spans over a duration exceeding 30 years. Please access the internet and input the numerical data, which will yield your predetermined installment amount of $922.64. This encompasses regulations and interests but excludes obligations, insurance, and mortgage insurance (if necessary).

There are two alternative methods through which you can conduct an inspection of your own residence:

1. Your family home forever. Some individuals may propose acquiring a residence that falls well within your means, with the rationale that future salary increments may diminish your desire to relocate to a more luxurious dwelling. If one were to presume that you have established a stable living arrangement and that your children are attending a preferred educational institution, it can be concluded that this approach is the most optimal method. You will achieve cost savings by

foregoing the expenditure associated with the sale of the property, typically ranging anywhere from 6 to 10%.

2. As a momentary speculation. If you have no objection to relocating periodically, considerable tax-exempt profits can be derived from the acquisition of a residential property, one's habitation in it for a substantial duration, and subsequent sale. All gains derived from this transaction will be exempt from taxation for amounts up to $250,000 ($500,000 for married individuals).

Due to the presence of these two methodologies, it is imperative that you make an informed decision regarding your personal and project objectives.

Delayed Gratification

The majority of individuals require immediate access to the more enjoyable aspects of life, such as high-end household appliances, luxury automobiles, and watercraft. While this assertion holds logical merit, achieving financial independence necessitates the exercise of prudence. I am not proposing that you prioritize efficiency, but rather that you adhere to a lifestyle within your financial limits.

There may arise instances wherein you must deliberate upon whether it is imperative to procure a new vehicle, or alternatively, ascertain if making minor repairs to your existing vehicle would suffice for a span of a few years without necessitating a new purchase. Although it may be challenging to make the decision to wait, you will experience greater happiness in the long run if you choose to do so.

Think about utility. Would you require means of transportation for commuting to your workplace? Indeed, you do. Would you prefer to commute to work in a $50,000 BMW or achieve a similar level of satisfaction with a $25,000 Ford?

Would you be interested in acquiring a television set? A significant number of individuals would concur by stating "Alright." Would you prefer a $10,000 home theater setup, or would a $500 Sony system offer comparable quality?

I may venture to surmise that you are cognizant of the solution.

Another aspect to consider is this: If it is necessary for you to support it, you may find yourself unable to afford it. This rule applies to all items, excluding only your initial automobile and real estate. When it comes to vehicle maintenance, it is advisable to allocate a portion of your monthly payment towards saving for your next vehicle over a period of two to three years. If one were to acquire automobiles that are a few years old, a substantial reduction of approximately 40% from the original price can be attained, while utilizing no more than 10% of the vehicle's lifespan. In my previous localities, a considerable proportion of my neighbors endeavored to outdo each other by purchasing expensive SUVs. Both my spouse and I drive recent vehicle models, however, we do not have any outstanding car loan payments. Our vehicles may not be the most extravagant, but they have been fully paid for. We derive greater satisfaction from the knowledge that our vehicle has been fully paid for, than from driving a more expensive vehicle that entails regular payments.

This hypothesis holds true for all objects or entities that experience degradation. What benefit is there in possessing the most exquisite television or audio system, if one must make recurring monthly payments that continuously depreciate in value?

I possess the ability to perceive your thoughts: It presents a greater challenge than one might anticipate. You have diligently earned your financial resources, and it is essential that you appreciate them... as is appropriate. Regardless, the period of satisfaction you will experience with your new extra large flat screen TV will be fleeting until a more contemporary model becomes accessible. By allocating those funds towards an investment property, you can establish a reliable source of income, which will afford you the opportunity to acquire a new television every two years. Is your current television capable of performing that function?

Upon successfully finalizing my initial land exchange and receipt of a credit for the improvements made, it is conceivable that I may have utilized the funds for miscellaneous expenditures. It would have been an extraordinary experience to acquire a more luxurious mode of transportation and indulge in an extensive shopping excursion. However, Cindy and I acknowledged that we had applied for the loan due to the properties being in exceptionally poor condition and in dire need of repairs and improvements. During the preceding six-month period, we made substantial investments into the properties, resulting in a nearly twofold increase in their rental yields. This allowed the properties to cultivate their positive cash flow and enhance their overall value. Following this, we engaged in the reevaluation of two or three properties and extracted funds for expenditure purposes. Taking everything into account, as a collective, we generate income... with the intention of utilizing it. However, it is imperative to exercise prudence to ensure that you are still pursuing your short-term and long-term objectives. We ultimately acquired everything necessary, albeit with a six-month delay; and in the interim, we successfully managed to increase the properties' overall value.

We devised an exceptionally intelligent solution: properties that served both our own needs and the new television.

Why Always Fail

We have thoroughly explored techniques to ease your foray into real estate investment, encompassing elements such as leveraging your strengths, aligning with your natural aptitudes, and employing a strategic approach to determine the most suitable real estate investment path towards achieving your objectives. However, we must also consider the final element of the cognitive framework conundrum: what precise factors are truly indispensable for attaining success?

One method to ascertain the requirements for your success is to temporarily pause your actions. Provided that you can avoid the associated pitfalls, you are considerably more likely to reach your desired destination, ideally encountering fewer obstacles in the process.

Error: Making an Investment Decision Without Sufficient Knowledge and Understanding

Children are not permitted to enter a pool without wearing proper flotation devices and being supervised by a responsible adult. They would suffocate. In essence, if one were to engage in land investment without prior exposure to any relevant practices, they would ultimately meet an unfavorable outcome. Furthermore, it is not feasible to acquire the skill of swimming with just a single lesson.

In fact, similar to numerous aspects of life, achieving success without haste truly prevails in the race. It holds particular significance in terms of acquiring education in real estate investing. It is imperative to allocate time towards acquiring essential information. If you fail to establish a sturdy foundation, you run the risk of jeopardizing everything by allocating it to a completely unreliable investment.

It does not necessitate a significant amount of time to acquire proficiency in the fundamentals. You should never be in such haste that you miss out on acquiring essential knowledge.

A minimal investment in education can significantly enhance preparedness and bolster the stability of one's investments. If I were tasked with selecting the primary fundamentals of real estate investment that every investor should understand, they would be:

variations in investment strategies and their respective alignment with specific objectives

assessment of the potential hazards associated with each approach and methods to alleviate those risk elements.

How to perform numerical calculations

market/city analyses

That is an exceedingly concise summarization, amenable to swift adaptation. If you take the time to acquire knowledge in all these four elements, you will position yourself significantly ahead of the majority of individuals involved in real estate investing, thereby increasing your chances of achieving success at a faster pace. While it does not guarantee that you will never experience failure, you are effectively minimizing the likelihood of failure or reducing its degree.

Chapter 2: Initiating an Airbnb Endeavor

Shall we commence the course? Upon completion of this course, you will possess a fundamental comprehension of both the initial steps involved in commencing this enterprise and the techniques to effectively persuade a landlord, thereby allowing you to embark on this business venture without actual property ownership.

There are numerous aspects to this business, however, I will make earnest efforts to provide you with comprehensive information.

Therefore, we will be examining:

The prospect - what renders Airbnb an advantageous business venture

The foundational aspects of the Airbnb enterprise

Comprehending the intricacies of temporary accommodations.

Take note of the local regulations governing short-term rentals within your city in order to conduct your business in compliance with the law.

Establishing your limited liability company

Examining the market for temporary accommodations

Strategies for conducting rental arbitrage

How to present a proposal to a property owner

Furnishing your property

Publishing your property on the Airbnb platform.

Advice on how to excel as a host on Airbnb, aiming for the esteemed title of Airbnb super host in order to attract a higher volume of bookings.

Lastly, allow me to provide you with some recommendations on how to implement automation within your enterprise, enabling it to operate independently rather than relying solely on your direct involvement.

Please note that the abbreviation STR refers to short-term rentals.

The Opportunity

Let us commence our discussion by delving into the factors that render Airbnb an exemplary business model. One initial thought is that no prior experience is necessary and minimal financial investment is required for initiation, thus rendering it accessible to individuals from various backgrounds. The initial investment ranges from $5,000 to $100,000, therefore, if you do not possess the necessary funds, alternative options include utilizing a credit card, procuring a business loan, or exploring opportunities to raise capital from friends and family. Furthermore, the business model is versatile, allowing for both part-time and full-time engagement. It will be ideal for individuals employed in traditional office hours (9-5) as they can conveniently pursue this opportunity alongside their main job, ensuring supplementary income. Furthermore, it is unnecessary to possess any form of licensure or academic qualification. An inquiry commonly raised regarding Airbnb pertains to the requirement of a real estate license for participation. It is important to note that no, possessing a real estate license is not necessary or compulsory in any way. It is possible that a business license may be required, but the specific regulations can vary depending on the jurisdiction in which you operate. The Airbnb enterprise operates entirely on automation, rendering it one of the most expeditious avenues of generating passive income, whether one finds it plausible or not.

Additionally, it is a business with low risk. This implies that once one has acquired the knowledge and skills of rental arbitrage, they have the ability to lease a property from a landlord. In the event that they determine the property to be unsuitable, they have the option to promptly return the property to its owner and discontinue the agreement. There is no necessity for you to remain with a property that you have financially invested in and purchased. If you are dissatisfied with the property you have leased, you have the option to terminate the agreement and withdraw. One notable advantage of this enterprise is its ability to be conducted remotely from any location across the globe. Suppose you embark on a journey to another location. In this scenario, you have the option to conveniently carry either your laptop or mobile device, enabling you to perform your professional tasks remotely, without the necessity of physically being present. Consequently, the absence of a physical workspace becomes a feasible reality. Essentially, it is not necessary to have a physical office space or employ staff in order to generate income, as one can achieve profitability without ownership of any real estate.

There are numerous advantageous aspects to this business model, and it is anticipated that a significant number of individuals will embark on it. Therefore, commencing your involvement sooner rather than later would be highly beneficial.

Chapter Six: An Exploration of Crypto Arts

In essence, cryptocurrency-based artworks are digital art forms that are treated with the same regard as physical art due to the ability to authenticate their ownership. Crypto art can be authenticated using non-fungible tokens (NFTs) just as a genuine Picasso artwork can be verified for its originality and provenance. Non-fungible tokens (NFTs) represent a distinctive entity that serves as an exclusive identifier associated with crypto artworks, effectively serving as a means to substantiate ownership of said item. It can be associated with various types of media, such as JPEGs, GIFs, MP4s, and even audio files. This document, which serves as evidence of the origin of the "source" file, is stored on the Blockchain, a universally accessible ledger accessible from any device.

What is the rationale behind the significant value attributed to Crypto Arts?

The value is based on the scarce nature and the concept that, due to the non-fungible token (NFT), the digital artworks cannot be duplicated. Another aspect is that individuals ascribe a monetary value to it. What is the reason behind the high valuation of particular rectangular cardboard pieces with photographs of baseball stars? Alternatively, one could consider the option of Beanie Babies. Alternatively, may I suggest considering the option of Pokemon cards? They possess intrinsic value as collectors highly esteem them. That comprises the entirety of the matter. The significance attributed to artwork by its collectors within the realm of cryptographic arts. Some collectors acquire crypto arts for the sole purpose of speculation, whereas others do so to support the creator or due to an emotional connection with the artwork.

It is important to recall that what Banksy is now celebrated for was initially categorized as vandalism. The payment for graffiti would never occur. The artwork produced by Banksy has attained a significant monetary worth, currently valued in the millions of dollars. Such is the capricious nature of the art industry.

Non-Fungible Tokens (NFTs), Digital Artworks, and the Virtual Reality Space

Due to their ability to facilitate digital ownership, Non-Fungible Tokens (NFTs) play a crucial role in the Metaverse. It is possible for individuals to acquire virtual artwork within the Metaverse and obtain a virtual residence for exhibiting said artwork. Given the NFTs' connection to the ETH Blockchain, their irreversibility and uniqueness are evident, ensuring that one's ownership of the artwork or property remains unquestionable by anyone.

The Metaverse is projected to foster a robust digital economy, with non-fungible tokens serving as its fundamental building blocks. The prevalence of micropayments in the gaming industry has seen a substantial increase, with their share in gaming earnings rising from twenty percent in 2010 to a significant seventy-five percent in 2020, thereby exemplifying their current widespread popularity. By the year 2025, it is projected that they will comprise a significant share of the total gaming revenue, accounting for approximately ninety-five percent, a mere four years from now.

Despite the nascent state of the metaverse concept, non-fungible tokens (NFTs) represent a crucial stride towards attaining its full potential. Decentralization holds great significance within the context of the Metaverse.

The convergence of the creative economy, virtual realms, cryptocurrencies, online social networks, and the reimagining of business models transpire within the realm of the Metaverse, non-fungible tokens (NFTs), and the sphere of digital arts. These particular subjects serve as representatives of the emerging digital era, characterized by its emphasis on self-expression, artistic endeavors, and social interactions.

Digital artists exemplify a novel vocation enabled by the widespread reach of the internet, one that possesses the potential for heightened profitability in comparison to conventional professions. Digital environments will bring about a transformation in the manner individuals interact and conduct their activities.

Roblox developers will populate the Metaverse with their virtual skyscrapers, parks, furnishings, and apparel. Individuals who engage in the development of Airtable applications in the present time will be instrumental in shaping the digital work environments of tomorrow. Merchants that create Cashdrop or Shopify stores will be able to create digital, 3D storefronts the next day. Talented individuals on TikTok will craft immersive digital entertainment ecosystems.

Furnish Your Rentals

One can derive enjoyment from commencing an Airbnb enterprise by expressing creativity and adorning the premises with tasteful furnishings. It is necessary to review the initial matter, which entails establishing a budget. It is advisable to exercise caution against overspending when attempting to furnish your unit, as doing so may prove unnecessary. Develop a predetermined financial framework specifically designated for furniture expenses.

Initially, I elucidated the methodology employed, although, to be frank, that constitutes the precise algorithm that must be employed. In the case of engaging in wrench arbitrage, it is necessary to multiply the monthly rent by a factor of 2.5.

Taking the initial illustration into account, let us consider the monthly rental cost of the property, which amounts to $1500. Depending on the type of property, we can multiply this amount by a factor of 2.5, resulting in a total of $3750. You may be curious about the origin of the value 2.5. Allow me to explain that through my experience and careful consideration, I have arrived at this particular value. Over a considerable period of time, I have consistently applied this formula, which has proven to be effective for me.

This approach may prove ineffective for your specific situation, potentially necessitating increased expenditure or additional purchases. If such is the circumstance, endeavor to refrain from exceeding this limit, as surpassing it may lead to complications.

At this point, it is necessary for you to select a theme for your Airbnb property. There is a vast array of themes available on the internet. You may conduct an online search using search engines such as Google to explore descriptors such as bohemian, earthy, modern, minimalist, and luxury, depending on the specific target audience you aim to reach. It would be beneficial if you adorned your Airbnb in such a manner.

Additionally, deliberating on the location to purchase your furniture is of paramount importance. There are numerous reputable establishments where one may choose to purchase furniture, such as IKEA, Walmart, Home Goods, Amazon, Hobby Lobby, Costco, Facebook Marketplace, and Craigslist. There are an ample number of available locations, however, if you are commencing your endeavor with limited financial resources, it would be prudent to consider procuring pre-owned furniture. The Facebook marketplace offers a wide selection of pre-owned furniture that boasts exceptional quality. Engaging in this activity would result in significant cost savings. Moreover, enhance the amenities available in your Airbnb to include offerings such as a coffee maker, essential kitchen supplies, quality towels, well-prepared bedding arrangements, a comfortable seating area, recreational activities, and so forth. Encourage ingenuity in this regard.

Once the furnishing of your Airbnb is complete, it is imperative that you engage the services of a professional photographer to capture visually appealing images of the furnished space. If individuals make an attempt to economize and employ their smartphones to capture images, their chances of receiving a large number of bookings might be compromised. This is attributable to the fact that some individuals tend to commit a blunder by employing their phones for photography, lacking the skill required to capture quality images. The photographs are captured without any additional lighting, showcasing the property in its natural state. A skilled photographer possesses the expertise to identify the most appealing features and enhance the space's attractiveness. Therefore, it is advisable to allocate the necessary funds for professional photography. It\\\'s all worth it. You shall not have cause for regret.

Once again, one must prioritize quality over quantity. If you possess a penchant for embellishing walls and furniture extensively, this might not align with your preferences as Airbnb accommodations typically necessitate ample space and an uncluttered aesthetic. No individual wishes to reside in an environment abundant with ornamental embellishments and furnishings.

The Metaverse And Music

At present, the consequences of Zuckerberg's remarkable ambition and project remain uncertain. However, with regard to music, it is conceivable that the most apparent innovation could pertain to live performances. Indeed, within this Metaverse, individuals have the opportunity to partake in genuine, immersive live concerts, make purchases of branded merchandise, or engage in distance-related music listening alongside companions. In brief, the potential ramifications could be substantial. We simply need to exercise patience for a few more years, after which we will be able to acquire further information. Or rather, live more.

The music industry is on the cusp of a burgeoning development: intertwined with the metaverse, a virtual reality realm enhanced with gaming elements, it presents considerable prospects for expanding music outreach to untapped demographics or engaging with fervent fan communities. Covering a range from Abba to Muse, this comprehensive overview showcases the artists capitalizing on the trend, along with their corresponding outcomes.

In a recent development, the highly renowned musical ensemble of the 1970s, Abba, has divulged their imminent comeback to the music industry. This resurgence entails the release of a fresh album after a four-decade hiatus, accompanied by an actual tour that will incorporate cutting-edge virtual technologies employing motion capture. These advancements will enable the artists to appear on stage as youthful avatars, owing to the process of de-aging.

The album, entitled Voyage, distributed through Universal Music, will serve as the focal point for the upcoming tour, commencing in May, which will be hosted in a specifically designed, technologically advanced venue in London.

The concept of the avatar has been previously employed, though in contemporary times it has been extensively utilized to orchestrate an event of such immense proportions, to such an extent that the esteemed Industrial Light & Magic, founded by

George Lucas, was selected to spearhead this ambitious endeavor.

Over 850 individuals collaborated in meticulously recreating the iconic peak of Abba's musical career. This feat was achieved through the utilization of sophisticated motion capture technologies, enabling the comprehensive scanning of every nuance and gesture exhibited by the septuagenarian musicians during their studio performance.

Producer Ludvig Andersson informed the BBC that Agnetha, Frida, Benny, and Bjorn, in the presence of approximately 160 cameras and nearly as many skilled animators in the field of visual effects, delivered flawless performances of every song featured in this show over a period of five weeks.

When witnessing this performance, one would come to realize that it is not a mere portrayal of Abba by four individuals, but rather an authentic representation of the actual band themselves.

The motion capture technology, which has already been employed in the film industry for an extended period, was also extensively showcased by Sony Music during the live event, featuring the talented artist Madison Beer, in three dimensions. The production offered fans the opportunity to fully engage in the artist's performance, utilizing on-demand visuals accessible via PlayStation VR and Oculus VR. The meticulously created scenario for this occasion beautifully transformed a standard television studio into a grand stadium-like event.

Why invest?

PART 1

Given your diligent efforts to earn money, it is entirely reasonable that you desire its growth to the fullest extent possible, as mentioned earlier.

You may have a set of objectives, either short-term or long-term, that you need to achieve. Maintaining focus on your objectives will ensure that you navigate in the correct direction.

It is essential to comprehend that by keeping your funds idle in a savings account, you are not maximizing their potential and potentially missing out on significant opportunities for financial expansion.

Who wouldn't be interested in augmenting their financial resources?

Furthermore, it is imperative to achieve a robust financial situation and possess the capability to forecast future circumstances. By depositing your funds, you can expedite the achievement of these objectives significantly.

Acquiring knowledge on the avenues for enhancing your financial resources and the tools at your disposal is the first stride you can undertake in the direction of improving your fiscal situation and realizing your aspirations.

Every speculation carries inherent risks. To have an opportunity to accumulate wealth, that is something with which you should be inclined to agree.

Certain investments carry lower risks and offer more guarantee of security, while there are also exceptional opportunities that promise significant returns but entail higher levels of risk. It is essential to carefully assess what aligns with your preferences.

It would be judicious to seek the guidance of a financial consultant, as they will take into account your comprehensive financial situation and be capable of advising whether the investment you are considering is suitable for you.

That does not imply that you should delegate the decision-making to someone else. After careful consideration, it can be concluded that the money in question belongs to you. It presents an opportune moment for you to embark upon the acquisition of knowledge and understanding pertaining to monetary matters, in order to make informed decisions that are most favorable to your personal circumstances.

Please seek the advice of a financial consultant, inquire about successful investors, conduct your own research, and subsequently you will be able to determine what is most optimal for your situation.

In terms of conjecture, you have the opportunity to invest your capital in order to explore and devise avenues for generating supplementary earnings.

Anticipating future circumstances is also of great importance. Engaging in advance retirement planning and allocating funds towards it will enable you to be in a considerably advantageous position when that opportune moment arises. You will not be solely reliant on your State's Pension, which frequently lacks the capacity to provide a sufficient income to sustain a comfortable lifestyle.

It is imperative to ensure that you have allocated sufficient funds to secure your children's education or to support their upward mobility in the real estate market as they reach adulthood.

In the event of an unfortunate occurrence, ensuring financial security for your family is also a goal that most individuals aspire to achieve.

Hence, investment inherently has the potential to exert a substantial influence on various facets of your life and aid you in augmenting your financial resources to attain your objectives. It is an erroneous assessment to assume that only affluent individuals have the capacity to make contributions. There is an extensive range of options available to you as well.

Another advantageous aspect of participating is that, in certain instances, you may also indirectly aid others, thereby negating the need for exclusive emphasis on your own participation in the advantages.

5. Not everything that shines is of value.

After an extended period of gradual accumulation, Jeremy eventually transitioned from managing dispersed single-family home rentals to consolidating his investment portfolio into two high-rise buildings. It took two decades to reach such a level of accomplishment, and the revenue generated by the two properties was astonishing. However, he remained somewhat dissatisfied.

Given his background as a business appraiser, he had encountered a vast array of real estate transactions throughout his professional tenure, and he strongly believed that there were considerably more promising investments on the horizon. He had been informed, by affluent individuals in the vicinity, about the revered objective of properties that generate exceptional income with minimal administrative challenges. In fact, having transitioned from single-family homes to condominiums, he now aspires to progress further.

Although Jeremy received a substantial income from the rental of the lofts, he complained to his partner about the headaches that accompanied the management of such a large number of units. Over the course of several years, he had encountered multiple on-site administrators for each property, and finding individuals who consistently provided excellent and reliable service proved to be a considerable challenge for him. Instead of benefiting from the inherent security provided by having numerous individual occupants, he sought to decrease the number of inhabitants for whom he was responsible. Jeremy believed that a minimalist approach would be more suitable for his needs. Reducing the number of occupants would result in fewer issues due to the diminished presence of individuals overall, thereby obviating the need to engage with potentially questionable individuals. In light of the imperative nature of completing the task promptly, he maintained the conviction that he should undertake it independently, irrespective of any assistance rendered.

Another factor that was causing frustration to Jeremy concerning his condominiums pertained to the types of tenants he was overseeing. They were residential occupants of a private nature, and a portion of them failed to remit their lease payments punctually. Due to his professional role as an appraiser, he observed the differential treatment exhibited by money managers concerning the settlement of their expenses. Organizations diligently settled their expenses promptly, as they operated with competent accountants and provided consistent compensation, unlike his regular apartment tenant who lacked the ability to balance a checkbook or manage financial responsibilities. Jeremy informed him that he intended to embark on a venture involving the reimagining of the realm of commercial real estate, specifically focusing on the leasing of properties to businesses.

An elderly widow approached him regarding conducting an inspection of her business premises. The property was exquisite; a top-tier office space located in the heart of the downtown area.

significant thoroughfare within the urban area. After her spouse's demise, Jeremy completed the examinations necessary to inherit his estate and assumed ownership of the property.

The aforementioned real estate, known as the Icon, had a limited number of tenants, including a highly notable attorney and an investment banking professional. Upon entering the structure, one was imbued with a sense of being on Wall Street, as evoked by the opulence of the marble, crystal fixtures, and grand oak finishes. Additionally, Jeremy had developed a strong fascination with the property.

He inquired about the rationale behind the widow's need for an evaluation, to which she replied that her intention was to engage in a sale. Jeremy displayed a wide, jovial smile that extended from ear to ear. This opportunity had been the object of his pursuit, given his awareness of her property ownership free of any encumbrances. Consequently, he saw the potential to arrange owner financing, thus circumventing the need for a traditional bank loan. He asked if it would be an incompatible scenario to discuss making a proposal, and she agreed that if another appraiser provided a complimentary valuation, she would be willing to negotiate a deal with him in order to circumvent the fees associated with listing with a broker. Additionally, her deceased partner had been acquainted with him for numerous years and consistently spoke highly of him.

This served as a commendable demonstration of a lucrative transaction in the realm of commercial real estate that took place outside the conventional market. Jeremy proposed a particular appraiser whom he believed would impartially evaluate the property, without favoring either party. Once the evaluation was completed, the widow and Jeremy negotiated a price that was approximately equivalent to the appraisal fee. Furthermore, right from the outset, Jeremy had foreseen obtaining a loan.

Jeremy anticipated that obtaining the loan would be relatively effortless, as he approached a pair of reputable financial institutions known for their preference towards high-end commercial establishments. However, he was taken aback by the fact that all of them rejected him. Undoubtedly, the Icon was attaining the financial resources that the lenders desired; however, there existed certain concerns that had instilled fear among these financial institutions. One possible reason was that maybe the primary lessee had a lease agreement that was due for renewal promptly. The main concern revolved around Jeremy himself. He had never owned any establishments of commerce. The breadth of his total assets and other financial details fell short of the expectations they had.

Unfazed by the setback, Jeremy approached the widow once again, suggesting the option of her approaching the bank for proprietor financing, given that he made a substantial down payment and agreed to refinance in the future.

3 years. What proved instrumental for Jeremy's success was his exemplary reputation for consistently fulfilling all his duties. She agreed.

In order to obtain the initial installment, Jeremy is required to sell the superior of his two apartment complexes. He intends to sell the additional assets and utilize the proceeds to engage in a 1031 exchange for the acquisition of this new property. This was a universal approach acquired through the entirety of his years in the real estate industry. Jeremy's expertise in land surpassed that of an amateur, making him remarkably knowledgeable in this domain.

Disposing of the condominium property would be remarkably straightforward owing to its remarkably robust positive cash flow and the diligent upkeep it has received. He had no requirement to make it accessible. He promptly contacted a select group of associates and expeditiously received a comprehensive offer at the listed price.

According to the data presented, the mathematical calculations did not appear to be as promising. The prospective property he intended to purchase failed to generate an equivalent amount of revenue compared to the existing high-rise he was in the process of selling. Jeremy considered that the reduction in issues related to managing only a few unquestionable tenants would outweigh the decrease in monthly revenue. Furthermore, the aforementioned property was situated in the most desirable sector of the district. He was making an offer to purchase Park Place by paralleling it to Kentucky Avenue, inspired by the popular board game Monopoly.

Upon the culmination of the entire arrangement, he assumed ownership of the Icon, utilizing

The amount of $600,000 was derived from the proceeds of the sale of his high-rise property, while the remaining $1 million was funded by the widowed proprietor. Jeremy believed he had presented himself as a proficient financial expert. He walked with a slightly heightened posture and spoke with a somewhat increased level of confidence. Each time he drove past, he had to exert pressure on his mind, as he found it hard to believe that he was actually the proud owner of the Icon.

Immediately, the alleviation of migraines resulting from no longer managing his previous apartment complex had considerably reduced the number of details he was required to attend to. Nevertheless, it was at that juncture when he discovered that establishments categorized as class A also encountered similar board-related challenges. As an example, the elevator ceased operation during regular business hours on a given day. Due to his lack of prior experience addressing such a matter, he was unprepared to promptly resolve it. Several days had elapsed before the issue was eventually resolved, by which time the resident of the venture banking firm was infuriated and contemplating legal action due to the inability of a few affluent clientele to access the staircase.

Having a highly influential attorney residing within the community proved to be a source of apprehension, as this individual possessed the ability to initiate legal proceedings at a moment's notice for even the most trivial matters. The situation became overly trivial, with the lawyer expressing dissatisfaction over individuals occupying his parking space, even though there were no officially designated parking spots.

for anybody. In order to appease him, Jeremy had a sign printed with an authoritative tone, designating the location for the lawyer. Nonetheless, subsequently the investment bankers expressed dissatisfaction regarding the absence of designated parking spaces exclusively for their use. Jeremy struggled to cope with it. These proficient finance managers exhibited a level of incompetence surpassing that of his condominium tenants.

Subsequently, Jeremy discovered that not everything that glimmers holds intrinsic value. The economy experienced a period of contraction, leading to the dissolution of various organizations. To his astonishment and dismay, the tenacious venture banking occupant was experiencing a collapse. Almost instantaneously, one of the two vital occupants within his ownership had disappeared; rendered insolvent and failing to fulfill their obligation of paying rent. Despite the high quality of the space, companies were making extra efforts to prepare for the worst effects of the economic downturn, making it exceptionally difficult to find a new tenant.

The attorney also delivered unexpected news to Jeremy, informing him that he would not be renewing the lease due to the departure of the investment banking tenant. Jeremy discovered that the attorney had acquired a segment of his clientele from the investment bank, and in order for his legal practice to continue prospering, a relocation to a new building where independent enterprises could contribute to managing his business became imperative. Jeremy steadfastly refused to embrace such reasoning, given the prevailing tendency among lawyers to refrain from contriving enduring assignments based on personnel transferring from neighboring firms. However, considering the imminent departure of the attorney in the next 8 months, Jeremy would be required to find a replacement tenant in order to avoid bearing the financial burden of the entire building, as the current tenants only occupy a mere 20% of the premises.

The decline persisted for a few more years. Throughout that period, Jeremy consistently failed to occupy both of the two principal vacancies. He employed all the positive earnings generated by his alternative apartment complex to satisfy the monthly obligations of the Icon. However, despite his efforts, this proved insufficient and shortly thereafter, he commenced to lag behind in making his payments. He reached out to each financial institution, seeking their assistance, and encountered a consistent lack of enthusiasm for a business involvement of 20% amidst a period of economic recession.

In the final outcome, the widow ultimately relinquished her claim and Jeremy incurred a significant financial loss, including the forfeiture of the property and the $600,000 invested. It concluded as a profoundly disheartening outcome of what initially began as a remarkable achievement in his professional pursuits. Moreover, to compound an already arduous circumstance, the high-rise property that he had sold exhibited unwavering resilience throughout the downturn, exacerbating the situation. Certainly, it would have been highly lucrative for Jeremy if he had not only purchased the Icon property, but also retained ownership of his apartment complex. This is evident from the fact that many homeowners who had lost their homes due to foreclosure opted to rent apartments. Consequently, Jeremy's cash flow would have significantly improved, surpassing previous levels.

Controlling the Cognitive Processes of the UI Investor

Part 3/3

Further Calming The Mind

In addition to regulating the amygdala, the center responsible for our instinctual fight or flight reaction, we require further assistance in quelling the UI Investor's Brain, specifically through the activation of serotonin and oxytocin.

Serotonin is a chemical compound that fulfills a diverse range of roles within the human physiological system. It is occasionally referred to as the euphoria-inducing compound due to its positive impact on overall well-being and happiness.

Oxytocin is produced by the posterior pituitary gland, a small gland located at the inferior part of the brain, referred to as the hypothalamus. It is occasionally referred to as the "cuddle hormone" or the "love hormone" due to its secretion during moments of snuggling or social bonding.

The techniques delineated in the preceding chapter, which I employ to subdue the cognitive processes of the UI investor, are:

Aerobic exercise

Listening to music

Allow me to present two additional techniques you may wish to consider implementing:

Drawbacks Of Investing In Low-Value Stocks

On numerous occasions, it has been observed that the value of stocks plummeted drastically, descending from 100 rupees to a mere 5 rupees, as a result of unfavorable news concerning the implicated company or due to fraudulent activities or scams conducted by said company.

A considerable number of investors exhibit the inclination to purchase the shares at a valuation of 5 rupees with the expectation of subsequently selling them at 10 rupees, thereby attaining a substantial 100% return on investment.

The enticement of quick profits compels them to acquire assets of minimal value, such as low-priced stocks or excessively leveraged out-of-the-money options, owing to their affordability and potential for substantial gains. If the aforementioned approach proves successful, substantial remuneration should be granted. Indeed, I concur with your statement. However, it is important to note the significantly limited likelihood of this venture yielding substantial financial returns. The likelihood of these trades proving successful, however, is highly improbable, thus it can be deduced that they possess a minimal probability.

Additionally, individuals who invest in low-value stocks or purchase options with a price ranging from 4-5 rupees typically possess a limited amount of capital and may, on occasion, be prepared to jeopardize their entire investment. Consequently, this renders their trade an endeavor fraught with high levels of risk. The essence of profitable speculation can be traced back to a handful of fundamental factors, which may appear straightforward in theory but prove to be challenging in execution. These variables pose a minimal risk and are highly probable, accompanied by a reasonable level of leverage.

Allow me to recount the tale of a mystical being enclosed within a vessel. Imagine stumbling upon an enchanted bottle, within which resides a genie capable of granting your every desire. He arrives with a proposition. You are obligated to purchase any share of their choosing, under the condition that following the purchase, you must subsequently sell the same shares to another party at a price lower than your initial purchase price. Failure to adhere to this requirement will result in severe consequences administered by the genie.

What course of action do you intend to pursue now? It would be highly unlikely for you to purchase a share valued at one paisa because its resale potential at a lower price to other individuals would be severely restricted. It is not feasible for you to offer a price of two paisa, as it is widely understood that the genie's conditions are well-known and no one would be inclined to engage in a transaction at such a significantly lower rate. In a similar vein, it would be unlikely for you to purchase the share for three paisa, as you would be unable to sell it to anyone for two paisa due to the absence of potential buyers. The aforementioned line of reasoning can be extrapolated to include fractions such as four, five, six paisa, and so forth, ultimately leading to the inevitable conclusion that this share should not be purchased at any cost. Nevertheless, there exist individuals who knowingly make purchases at exorbitant prices despite the potential inability to subsequently sell the shares due to the imminent downfall of the company, with the share price merely serving the purpose of facilitating trade. Those who make a purchase will not have the ability to resell the product at a higher price.

This occurred with the DSQ software share, which experienced substantial trading activity at a price of Rs. 3000 per share, but subsequently declined to 5 Rupees within a short span of time. There was an absence of potential buyers for that particular share in the market, resulting in the cessation of its trading activity.

In conclusion, it can be stated that this inexperienced trader employs maximum leverage in trading activities characterized by the lowest likelihood of success and the highest degree of risk. The mathematical calculations demonstrate superior performance when adopting a strategy that minimizes risk, maximizes likelihood of success, and employs a moderate level of leverage.

Education and Career Paths

Initiate the commencement of the auditory accompaniment associated with the resurgence of temporal exploration to previous epochs. For centuries, women have predominantly occupied the role of homemakers, prioritizing the nurturing and upbringing of children within the confines of their own households. Although this has experienced a transformation in the past century, the opportunities available to women remain constrained by the scope of their acquired knowledge. In recent times, women have predominantly been educated for non-STEM (science, technology, engineering, and mathematics) professions. While careers in any of those aforementioned disciplines can certainly be highly fulfilling, possessing proficient numerical skills is imperative for achieving success in various aspects of life. Mathematics serves as the bedrock of financial knowledge, and financial literacy forms the basis for making sound investment decisions. Paradoxically, the construction of a house commences with the establishment of a foundation (mathematics), followed by the erection of walls (finance) and ultimately, the completion of the structure with the addition of a roof (investing). In order for a roof to function properly, it must be situated atop horizontal walls and supported by a stable foundation. Similar to a dwelling, an individual will not make a meaningful contribution or attain success in contribution without possessing a solid understanding of financial matters, rooted in a firm foundation of mathematical knowledge. It is unsurprising that women have historically exhibited a reluctance to engage in investment, given that a significant number of women have not been exposed to the fundamental principles of mathematics and financial comprehension that cultivate an understanding of the impact of investing.

It is noteworthy that women surpass men in their contributions, as evidenced by the data obtained from the aforementioned source (https 9adc98bf1d35a056). As one would anticipate, whenever the convergence of information and opportunity transpires, accomplishment can be attained. With a continued emphasis on encouraging women to pursue education and careers in STEM, the knowledge gap will diminish, thereby creating opportunities for a more profound understanding of finance and investment.

Why Does This Matter?

The gender disparity concerning investment aversion, access to education, wage inequality, and disparity in life expectancy warrants attention from individuals of all gender identities. For individuals of the male gender, the presence of a spouse, mother, sister, daughter, aunt, cousin, or female acquaintance within their familial or social spheres inevitably leads to a consequential impact. The burden of financial strain frequently falls upon the shoulders of those who provide for their family. According to a study conducted in January 2020 by the American Association of Retired Persons, it was discovered that approximately 32 percent of individuals in their middle age have rendered financial assistance to their parents at some point during the previous year. Taking a glimpse into the future, approximately 42 percent are of the opinion that they will extend financial assistance in the times to come. This issue affects individuals irrespective of their gender.

Where to Start

The adage "Knowledge is Power" holds significant weight and remains entirely applicable in the present context. Engage in independent learning concerning the power of contribution. Acquire knowledge on diverse factors that contribute to personal liberties. Some individuals often employ a financial planner who is compensated based on commissions to carry out this task, however, caution should be exercised regarding their method of remuneration. Monetary organizers who work on a commission basis can receive compensation if you choose to invest in specific ventures. However, it is likely that those endeavors would not be suitable for your specific financial situation. Seeking guidance from a financial advisor with expertise in expenses, such as a Certified Public Accountant (CPA) or a financial counselor who possesses firsthand knowledge of your specific financial situation, can provide you with the most sound and impartial advice to help you achieve your financial goals. If you happen to encounter the phrase, "I am not aware of a fee-based financial advisor," or "My CPA does not provide this service," it would be wise to seek an alternative and make a change.

Provide mutual support in order to facilitate the understanding and resolution of disparities among various sexual orientations. It is not feasible for all individuals to convene for the sole purpose of addressing an issue that only a subset of the population perceives. If you hold a position of authority, specifically if you possess a comprehensive understanding of the potential of investing, it is imperative that you impart knowledge to others. It is advisable to inform them that wealth does not necessarily require abundance, but rather, contributing is an essential factor for achieving wealth.

In the end, achieving liberation from the cycle of constant work rests upon one's financial means. Often, money is closely associated with power, but surrendering to its control can transform it into constraints. You have developed a strong affinity towards it. These bracelets are available in a variety of metals (nickel, silver, bronze, gold, and platinum) depending on the level of financial security required. Individuals who amass a seven-figure fortune may exhibit a stronger affinity for money compared to individuals earning a modest five-figure income. For example, a person could make $40,000 a year with living expenses of only $20,000 and have greater financial freedom than the platinum cuffed executive making one million dollars a year, whose annual expenses total one million five hundred thousand dollars. Irrespective of the compensation level, these individuals are subordinate to the power that money bestows upon them. Cash can take another structure, a superpower. This extraordinary ability serves as the catalyst that liberates individuals from the constant pursuit of material success, bestowing them with autonomy across all spheres.

At first, my belief was that the path to liberation from the monotonous routine of everyday life revolved around embracing an entrepreneurial persona. A business visionary asserts their concepts, determines their own schedule, and holds no obligation towards superiors, which enables limitless possibilities for income generation. While this may serve as the medium through which opportunities are achieved, it does not constitute the method itself. I discovered the method by harnessing the potent influence of financial resources. I have established a unique understanding of how cash operates that benefits me, rather than the other way around. Specifically, I acquire monetary assets that generate income during periods of repose. While my finances are being productively employed, I am successfully pursuing a predetermined goal, while also devoting quality time to my children. Given that I have provided you with the key, the question at hand pertains to whether you will unlock the superpower.

Determine Your Goals

Curiously, it is widely acknowledged that this step is often disregarded when individuals first embark on their journey into real estate investment. It should be evident that individuals may question the necessity of becoming an investor prior to embarking on it. However, there appears to be an inherent understanding for most individuals that being an investor can be highly astute and lucrative, thus they assume it to be a requisite without further inquiry.

If serving as a financial supporter is undeniably advantageous, why would individuals feel compelled to justify their decision to engage in such an endeavor? Response: It will be essential along the journey to comprehend the underlying motive behind your imperative need to engage in such an action. "It will be fundamental for two reasons:

1. Gaining insight into the rationale behind the necessity of your contribution is paramount.

Directly aligned with your investment objectives, comprehending your goals will enable you to make a more informed selection of the strategy that may be the most suitable for yourself and offer you the greatest probability of success.

2. When faced with challenging circumstances, as is inevitable, it is advantageous to maintain utmost clarity regarding the precise motives behind your endeavors, thereby ensuring that you remain driven to surmount

adversities and ultimately achieve your desired outcome.

If nothing else, obtaining the essential requirements can serve as a profound source of inspiration, compelling one to fully immerse oneself in this industry and make the journey into it even more exhilarating.

How would you ascertain a precise understanding of your specific requirements as a financial supporter? Financial resources are undoubtedly a prevalent aspect for individuals, however, it alone cannot serve as the guiding framework or sole motivator to overcome obstacles.

What will greatly aid you in achieving both of those objectives is the understanding of your underlying motivation.

currency. Subsequent to that, additional forms of cryptocurrency have been developed.

The cryptographic representation is the sole means by which ownership of cryptocurrency units can be established.

Alternative cryptocurrencies or altcoins encompass tokens, digital currencies, and various types of digital assets apart from bitcoin.

Altcoins often exhibit inherent differences when compared to bitcoin. Ethereum is globally recognized as the blockchain with the highest degree of efficiency and boasts the largest follower base among all alternative cryptocurrencies.

A blockchain is an ever-progressing inventory of records, known as blocks, that are interconnected and secured through cryptography.

According to the intended design, blockchains remain resistant to any form of alteration of their contained information. A blockchain provides the authentication of the coins associated with each digital currency. The majority of digital currencies are designed to gradually reduce the production of that currency, imposing a limit on the overall amount of money that will ever be in circulation.

The digital currency contained within a wallet is not associated with individuals, but rather with one or more specific keys.

Bitcoin owners' identities are not discernible, though all transactions are publicly accessible on the blockchain.

Cryptocurrencies are predominantly employed in sectors that exist independently from traditional banking and regulatory institutions, with transactions taking place primarily online.

Cryptocurrency transactions enable individuals to trade digital currencies for various assets, such as traditional fiat currencies or perform exchanges between different digital currencies.

Currently, there exist operational automated teller machines (ATMs) facilitating cryptocurrency transactions, with additional ones under development. One can employ a card, such as a charge/Visa, in order to withdraw funds and make payment for their purchases (although this option may not be widely accessible at present).

Cryptocurrency networks are characterized by a lack of regulation, a situation that has been criticized for providing opportunities for criminals to evade taxes and engage in money laundering.

Transactions carried out through the utilization and exchange of these alternative cryptocurrencies are independent of formal financial frameworks, thus facilitating the potential for tax evasion.

"Several prominent Cryptocurrencies include:

• Bitcoin. The most known crypto. Initially introduced in 2008 with subsequent utilization commencing in 2009.

• Ethereum. Otherwise called ETH. It possesses a decentralized coding platform that enables the development and execution of applications. The primary aim of Ethereum is to establish a decentralized framework for financial instruments, ensuring universal accessibility for individuals worldwide, irrespective of their personal attributes, nationalities, or religious affiliations. Ethereum is a platform that utilizes blockchain technology to facilitate the exchange of a cryptocurrency known as ether. At the moment, it ranks as the second-largest digital currency following Bitcoin.

- Litecoin. Otherwise called LTC. It possesses a higher rate of block generation, resulting in expedited transaction confirmation compared to Bitcoin. A growing number of merchants have started accepting Litecoin as a form of payment.

- Cardano. Otherwise called ADA. Still in preliminary stages. It aspires to become the global financial system by establishing decentralized financial products.

- Bitcoin Cash. Otherwise called BCH. It is capable of facilitating transactions at a faster pace in comparison to the Bitcoin organization. There are fewer instances of delays and the costs associated with processing are reduced.

• Stellar. Additionally, know and XLM. Designed to facilitate the integration of financial institutions for large-scale transactions. Significant transactions between banks and venture companies, which traditionally would necessitate several days and entail substantial financial outlays, can now be conducted almost instantaneously, devoid of intermediaries and incurring negligible costs for the parties initiating the transaction. It remains an accessible blockchain that can be utilized by anyone at present. The framework accounts for cross-border transactions involving various currencies. The organization anticipates that clients would possess Lumens in order to carry out transactions on the network.

• Binance Coin. Otherwise called BNB. It represents a platform wherein customers can engage in the trading of financial coins while utilizing BNB to facilitate the conversion of various digital currencies.

• Tether. Otherwise called USDT. An integral aspect of a consortium of stable coins entails pegging their value to a currency or some external benchmark, thus mitigating fluctuations in volatility.

• It strives to reduce price discrepancies in order to attract potential customers who may otherwise be hesitant. The cost of ties demonstrates a direct correlation with the value of the US dollar.

• Monero. Otherwise called XMR. It is a secure, confidential, and untraceable form of currency.

Conduct thorough research before incorporating cryptocurrencies into your investment portfolio. Cryptos are risky.

Engaging in investments pertaining to digital currencies entails a significantly speculative nature. This market exhibits remarkable volatility, and there exists a substantial possibility of significant financial setbacks.

Advantages of cryptos:

• Cryptocurrencies facilitate swift and cost-effective monetary transfers. This renders them highly sought-after for international monetary transactions.

• Cryptocurrencies are free from the control of experts and cannot be subjected to freezing.

• There are those who hold the belief that they will serve as the currency of the future.

• Certain allies appreciate the manner in which digital currency circumvents the involvement of national banks in managing the supply of physical currency, as these banks have historically displayed a tendency to...

erode the value of currency via inflation

• Cryptocurrencies possess a global nature, thereby conferring an equitable value across nations.

- Cryptocurrencies are transacted peer-to-peer on the internet, eliminating the need for an intermediary.

- Bitcoin exchanges offer a level of anonymity and confidentiality that ensures the identities of individuals involved remain undisclosed.

- Minimal, insignificant charges

- Fast

- Non-inflationary

- Payment freedom

- Central legislatures are unable to revoke it.

Disadvantages of cryptos:

- The ultimate outcome of digital currency is not assured. • The ultimate destiny of digital currency remains uncertain. • The final verdict on the future of digital currency cannot be established. Investors who wish to make projections in this market are advised to adhere to the prominent cryptocurrencies, including bitcoin, ethereum, and litecoin.

• Due to the intangible nature of digital currencies and the absence of a centralized storage facility, a record balance can be depleted. In the event that a client misplaces the private key associated with their wallet, it is noteworthy that the digital currency they possess cannot be restored or retrieved.

• Fraudsters can also hijack someone's mobile account by impersonating an account holder.

• Very speculative

• Numerous individuals still lack awareness about cryptocurrencies.

• Potential interference by governmental entities. • Potential obstruction by governmental authorities. • Possible hindrance caused by government involvement. They can be banned.

• Absence of remedy

• Employed for illicit tax evasion or the shadow economy.

In order to acquire digital currencies, it is necessary to possess a wallet, which refers to an online application designed to securely store your currency.

You can create a transaction history, and subsequently transfer actual currency for the purpose of purchasing cryptocurrencies.

Exclusively make use of a wallet provided by a reputable company. Do your research. Coinbase and Binance are recognized as two of the largest global platforms for exchanging bitcoin.

In the event that you require the acquisition of bitcoin and other cryptocurrencies, followed by subsequent sale, it is to be expected

Some of the charges include, but are not limited to, exchange expenses, deposit charges, withdrawal charges, and transaction fees.

A Brief Real Estate Educational Overview in 30 Seconds

Prior to delving into the narrative of my arrival, it is advisable that we establish an appropriate rhythm by means of a brief 30-second introduction. I am uncertain whether you are approaching this book as a proven investor or as a skeptical enthusiast. The most profound advice I have ever received was when an individual with extensive expertise attempted to condense their wisdom accumulated over many years into a brief exchange with me.

Currently, I anticipate one thing: your commitment to embracing a lifestyle characterized by self-sufficiency and liberation from the monotonous routines of modern life. Unaffected by its influence (as is everyone else), except genuinely sincere in relation to it. Presuming that to be the case, it is highly likely that you have conducted sufficient research prior to discovering this book, thereby recognizing that real estate holds immense importance in the realm of optimal wealth creation strategies for the majority of individuals.

When it comes to land, there are numerous strategies for securing a seat at the table. Every option presents its own set of benefits as well as risks and disadvantages, among which vacation rentals are included.

I had the opportunity to apply a discount—something I engaged in extensively over a prolonged period—resulting in exceptional financial gains. Regardless of the extent to which you are prepared to dedicate your efforts towards becoming a full-fledged expert, vigilantly observe the market conditions on a consistent basis, and assume the responsibility of taking calculated deals, it can indeed yield favorable outcomes. However, I cannot endorse this to individuals who engage in investing on a part-time basis due to their employment or business commitments, as they may not have sufficient time available to adequately manage their investments. It requires a significant amount of time and effort, as one must consistently work diligently to identify properties located at significant distances that can be offered to other investors at discounted rates.

You have the option to engage in the practice of buying properties in need of repair, improving them, and selling them for profit—I myself pursued this endeavor and achieved considerable financial success in the process. It is a particularly enjoyable model as it allows for the thorough refinement of a concept, thereby capturing its enhanced value. Furthermore, provided that you are able to commit yourself to doing it on a full-time basis, obtain the necessary funding, make astute investments, and exert significant effort, it has the potential to yield positive outcomes.

Additionally, there exists the option of long-term leases, which is commonly employed by employed individuals or organizations due to its potential for part-time engagement. However, this is an extensive procedure, rife with inconveniences such as late-night toilet repairs, and one that many aspiring kingdom builders ultimately abandon, primarily due to its overwhelming frustration (I too succumbed to this)."

These are the principal ones that you become acquainted with. There are several other categories that we did not explore, such as progress, innovation, multi-family and many more.

The crucial factor lies in the fact that the champions exhaust a significant portion, if not all, of their time in pursuit of discounted bargains. Moreover, they manage a substantial level of risk and must either rely on the fruits of their labor or patiently await a payout over a span of 20 to 30 years.

However, there exists an alternative approach—one that offers the benefits of a robust, sustained strategy applicable to any market condition, be it positive or negative. Furthermore, this approach consistently generates income and possesses an additional lifestyle advantage, propelling individuals towards success at a significantly accelerated pace compared to any other model available.

This vehicle is hereby referred to as Lifestyle Assets.

Diverse Range Of Choices And Their Stylistic Variations

Regardless of the chosen style or strategy employed by options day traders, it is essential to consistently consider three crucial components. The following elements are:

Liquidity pertains to the ease and expeditiousness with which an option or any other asset can be purchased or sold without causally impacting the prevailing market price. Liquid options are considered more preferable to options day traders due to their higher degree of tradability. Illiquid options pose an increased challenge to the seamless execution of a trader's ability to initiate or terminate their position.

This elongates the duration required to conclude the implicated transactions, consequently resulting in potential financial detriment for the options day trader.

Price sensitivity: This refers to the degree of responsiveness of the assets underlying the options to fluctuations in prices caused by external factors. Certain assets exhibit higher levels of volatility when compared to others. Stocks and Cryptocurrencies are subject to significant price fluctuations. Fluctuations in market volatility significantly influence the profitability of individuals engaged in day trading of options.

Trading Volume: This pertains to the quantity of options being exchanged within a given time frame. The level of trading activity, as reflected by the volume, provides valuable insights into the market's perception of an asset's price movement, serving as a reliable gauge of the asset's market appeal. Traders tend to be more inclined to pursue an option when there is a greater volume associated with it. The inclusion of volume contributes to the determination of open interest, defined as the aggregate count of active options. The active options have not undergone liquidation, exercise, or assignment. Failure to promptly act on options as an options trader can result in adverse circumstances, subsequently leading to unwarranted financial losses. It is essential for an options trader to consistently demonstrate astute awareness in order to timely close options positions.

In order to capitalize on the available choices for options day trading presented below, it is imperative for the day trader to possess a comprehensive understanding of these aspects and the strategic methods with which they can be employed to their benefit.

Exploring Opportunities in Day Trading Strategies

Breakout refers to the phenomenon whereby prices deviate from their customary price range upon market entry. In order for this trading approach to yield favorable outcomes, there must be a corresponding augmentation in trading volume. There exist multiple variations of breakouts, however, we shall address one highly prevalent type, labeled as support and resistance breakouts.

The support and resistance methodology delineates the level at which the corresponding asset price ceases its downtrend (support) and the level at which the corresponding asset price ceases its uptrend (resistance). The day trader will initiate a long position if the price of the corresponding asset surpasses the resistance level. Conversely, the options day trader will initiate a short position in the event that the correlating asset falls beneath the established support level. As evidenced, the trader's position is contingent upon whether the asset finds support or encounters resistance at the aforementioned price level. Upon surpassing the conventional price obstacle, there is typically an uptick in volatility for the asset. This typically leads to the associated asset price moving in the direction of the breakout.

When considering this approach to trading, it is essential for the options day trader to meticulously analyze their entry points and exit strategies. The customary approach to market entry relies on whether the prices are poised to surpass the resistance level or fall below the support level. The day trader will assume a bearish stance in the event that the price is deemed to be surpassing the resistance level. A bullish strategy is commonly employed when prices are poised to conclude below the support level.

Exit strategies necessitate a more refined and intricate approach. The options day trader must take into account historical performance and analyze chart patterns in order to ascertain an appropriate price target for exiting their position. After attaining the target, the day trader can conclude the trade and reap the earned profit.

Strategies For Investing In The Real Estate Market

Does Real Estate Investment Align with Your Goals and Interests?

The real estate sector is a multifaceted industry that entails numerous legal, financial, and interpersonal complexities.

Are you prepared to embark on this challenging venture? Prior to commencing, kindly take into consideration the following pivotal inquiries.

1. What is the extent of your financial investment capacity?

Participating in the real estate market requires the utilization of financial resources. The initial financial expenditure necessary to acquire a house may vary significantly or insignificantly. Nevertheless, once you assume ownership of the property, you are legally bound to fully reimburse the loan entirety. Conduct a thorough assessment of your own financial situation to ascertain whether you possess the means necessary to engage in investment activities. What kind of

money do you have? What is the extent of your financial capacity to sustain debt and bear interest expenses? Take into account the potential gains you could receive

lose.

2. Are you prepared to assume risks?

Risk and capital are inherently intertwined. To what extent are you prepared to assume peril? A substantial decrease in return on a minimal financial contribution

exerts a significantly more pronounced influence compared to an equivalent financial setback for an affluent investor possessing substantial resources. Although engaging in risky ventures can be exhilarating, it is imperative to maintain financial transparency and carefully contemplate the potential consequences.

level of risk that aligns with your comfort zone. Do you naturally

Do you tend to exhibit a preference for embracing risks, or do you lean towards being more risk averse? Having a strong awareness of your personal boundaries is vital for achieving success.

3. What are your overarching financial objectives in the long run?

Would you prefer to make an investment aimed at preserving cash or one that focuses on maximizing returns within a minimal timeframe? Consider the time,

Financial resources, as well as potential hazards, associated with each particular circumstance. Take a rational approach. A 15 percent gain within a short span of weeks is unattainable. If one desires a substantial return, it usually involves a

A more formal way to express the same idea could be: "Extended time commitment results in a prolonged period of financial investment." Volatility in property values can rapidly expose individuals to heightened risks.

4. Do you believe you possess the requisite qualifications?

To achieve success in the field of real estate investment, it is imperative to possess a high level of attention to detail, a propensity for rapid acquisition of knowledge, and exceptional interpersonal abilities. It is imperative to possess the requisite self-discipline and organizational skills to discern and prioritize one's knowledge gaps, and subsequently dedicate oneself to their acquisition and application.

5. What is the time allocation you can make available for this task?

Take into account the amount of time you are able to allocate towards the daily responsibilities requisite for achieving success within this company. You\\\'ll need to

Dedicate a substantial amount of time to studying and acquiring knowledge about the workings of the business initially. One will be required to invest considerable effort in addressing matters pertaining to legal obstacles, zoning and municipal concerns, insurance, tax implications, contractual agreements, market analysis, and financial aspects when embarking on any business endeavor.

If, after due consideration of these inquiries, your interest in pursuing real estate investment remains undiminished, we extend our congratulations to you. We believe that this avenue of endeavor ranks among the most captivating and promising means of securing a livelihood.

Engage In Investment With Well-Defined Objectives

Most individuals tend to develop an inclination towards investing during a similar stage of their lives. There is a strong probability that a significant portion of the readership shares a similar age range of approximately ten years, and it can be reasonably assumed that their socioeconomic circumstances exhibit only minor variations. When working with a collective of individuals who fall within a similar age range, it is often observed that they share common objectives, albeit their motives for investment can vary significantly. Irrespective of one's marital status or the number of children they have, it is essential to ascertain the underlying reasons for investing before embarking on the journey of acquiring investment knowledge.

There exist numerous rationales for desiring to make investments for the future; however, a select few prevalent ones include ensuring financial stability during retirement and accumulating funds for a child's further education. Your objectives may lean towards recreational activities, where you aspire to have the means to enjoy lengthier trips to high-end destinations. All of these goals serve as excellent catalysts for your interest in investment, however, each necessitates a distinct approach. Are you seeking financial resources for immediate or enduring periods? Are you seeking the ability to promptly withdraw invested funds, or are you comfortable with leaving them untouched in an account for a duration of ten to fifteen years? These inquiries will play a crucial role in determining the most suitable investment plan for your needs.

A Ubiquitous Investment Objective.

Over the course of time, it is inevitable that one's investment objectives will evolve; however, we can commence by considering a common aspiration shared by many: saving for the future of our children. Commencing to allocate funds for higher education in 2016 may seem intimidating. Given the continuous escalation of higher education expenses, it is projected that the anticipated expenditure for sending a child to a private university in 2034 will amount to $378,000. The observed increase in price can be perceived as substantial, and it is indeed accurate to acknowledge this. Nevertheless, it is important to note that costs have consistently been escalating by four percent annually over an extended period of time. Although public schools provide a commendable standard of education at a comparatively lower expense, it is worth noting that the cumulative amount over a span of eighteen years can still reach up to $168,000.

It may appear implausible that prices would persistently escalate over the course of the next eighteen years, leading one to question the existence of a theoretical threshold. This viewpoint has been observed among multiple individuals, leading them to presume that there will be an escalation in tuition fees, yet asserting that a constant annual increase of four percent over the next twenty years is highly improbable. Regrettably, the prospect of government intervention in college pricing appears improbable, or at the very least carries little promise for reducing the cost of education. There are two primary factors that significantly contribute to the substantial rise in tuition fees. Firstly, the escalating demand for a college education as a means of attaining lucrative employment, and secondly, the accessibility of loans extended to the majority of students aspiring to enroll in American universities.

Currently, the interest rates on federal higher education loans are significantly low, allowing borrowers to repay their loans over an extended period of multiple decades. They are an indispensable requirement for millions of American families; nevertheless, they also constitute the primary reason for the exorbitant costs associated with education. The primary factor driving the significant surge in costs is the notable rise in the proportion of students achieving a collegiate or advanced level of education. These assured educational loans ensure that irrespective of the field of study pursued by a student, they will secure funding with a guarantee. Presently, there is an insufficient provision of information to students regarding the level of financial remuneration they can anticipate to receive upon completion of their degree. The underlying idea is that student loans play a crucial role in ensuring the future prospects for your child, while simultaneously being a contributing factor to the high cost of their college education. In the event of a reduction in the student loan program, its efficacy will be diminished, rendering it less advantageous for both you and your offspring, necessitating alternative means of financing their education. If the current program persists, it would facilitate unfettered acquisition of loans that grant unrestricted educational opportunities, albeit perpetuating a yearly increase in tuition costs by approximately four percent. In either scenario, it is imperative to make adequate preparations; if you intend to contribute towards your child's higher education expenses, it is advisable to commence saving.

Objectively speaking, the competence in evaluating stocks is undeniably the most essential skill of all. Investors should not hold the expectation of amassing wealth solely by relying on gambling or blindly following the crowd. In the event that one fails to assess the present value and the future potential of the stock, substantial financial losses may ensue. This chapter is exclusively devoted to assisting you in acquiring understanding on the process of determining the worth of a stock and evaluating its performance, as well as providing strategies to optimize your investment returns and minimize risks. Moreover, it should be noted that value investing, much like other investment approaches, entails certain inherent risks.

It is imperative to gain insight into the potential risks associated with engaging in value investing. In the immediate term, there is potential for losses;

however, we are focused on pursuing absolute returns in the foreseeable future through the execution of this strategy.

Nonetheless, the outcome is contingent upon the selection of stocks. Presented below are several risks that necessitate mitigation in order to attain triumph.

Efforts should be made to mitigate the risks associated with investments.

1. NOT UNDERSTANDING FIGURES

It poses a significant risk, as I previously indicated. No individual can effectively make prudent decisions without first perusing the financial reports and comprehending the company's unique selling proposition, market demand, innovative initiatives, and long-term strategic vision. I have observed that the majority of individuals base their decisions on the financial statements, which aligns with the essence of value investing. However, it is imperative to ensure that you possess the most up-to-date and comprehensive information pertaining to the company.

Acquire the ability to discern the numerical data, and you will effectively mitigate a significant peril of financial detriment. Prioritize acquiring proficiency in analyzing financial reports before embarking upon investment ventures. The comprehensive information that you seek can be located within the footnotes section of either the 10-K or 10-Q reports. Look closely!

In the immediate term, the market functions as a mechanism for collective decision-making. However, ultimately, it serves as a device for assessing and comparing."

Ben Graham

2. TREMENDOUS GAINS AND LOSSES

The inherent volatility of the stock market renders it capricious even to the most seasoned observers. Hence, it is possible for multiple occurrences to occur that could potentially enhance a company's revenue or deplete their profits. Examples of occurrences include litigation, scientific inquiry and progress, organizational changes prompted by natural catastrophes, and additional scenarios.

Companies do not possess absolute authority over such circumstances; nonetheless, they may entail a sudden upturn or a significant downturn for you in your capacity as an investor. Do not give consideration to these matters during the process of analysis and decision-making, as they lack consistency. The assessment of the company's performance shall entail the omission of such incidents. It is acceptable to exercise discernment and prepare for unforeseen circumstances; however, it is important not to anticipate or rely on them.

Why are non-fungible tokens significant?

Non-fungible tokens represent a progression beyond the comparatively straightforward concept of cryptocurrencies. Contemporary financial systems comprise advanced trading and lending mechanisms for a variety of asset categories, spanning from real estate to lending agreements to works of art. Through the facilitation of digital representations of tangible assets, Non-Fungible Tokens (NFTs) mark a significant advancement in the reinvention of this foundational framework.

Indeed, the notion of digital representations of physical assets is not unprecedented, nor is the utilization of distinctive identification. Nonetheless, when these notions are amalgamated with the advantages of an impervious blockchain technology for smart contracts, they become a formidable catalyst for transformative progress.

Arguably, the most conspicuous advantage of NFTs lies in their facilitation of market efficiency. The process of transforming a tangible asset into a digitized form enhances efficiency and eliminates intermediaries. The utilization of Non-Fungible Tokens (NFTs) to depict artistic creations in both digital and physical forms on a blockchain technology eliminates the necessity of intermediaries, enabling artists to establish direct connections with their respective audiences. They also have the capability to enhance operational procedures. For instance, the utilization of a non-fungible token (NFT) in the case of a wine bottle would facilitate seamless engagement of various stakeholders within the supply chain, enabling efficient monitoring of its origin, production, and sale across the entirety of the procedure. Ernst & Young, a renowned consulting firm, has successfully devised a similar solution for one of its clientele.

Non-fungible tokens also serve as a superb solution for identity management. Let us examine the scenario involving physical passports that are required to be presented at each point of entry and departure. Through the transformation of individual passports into Non-Fungible Tokens (NFTs), each possessing distinctive identifying features, it becomes feasible to streamline the procedures of entry and departure across various jurisdictions. In addition to the foregoing use case, NFTs can also find application in the realm of digital identity management.

NFTs have the capacity to democratize investing through the process of fractionalizing tangible assets, such as real estate. It is significantly more convenient to distribute a digital property among multiple stakeholders as compared to a physical one. The ethically bound concept of tokenization is not limited solely to real estate, as it can be applied to diverse assets, including artwork. Therefore, it is not always necessary for a painting to have a singular owner. The digital counterpart possesses the capability to have multiple owners, wherein each individual assumes responsibility for a portion of the painting. Such arrangements have the potential to enhance its value and boost its revenues.

The creation of new markets and investment opportunities represents the most promising potential for NFTs. Contemplate a parcel of real estate subdivided into multiple divisions, each of which encompasses distinct characteristics and property types. One of the sectors could be located adjacent to a shoreline, whereas another may consist of a multifaceted entertainment complex. Furthermore, an additional sector comprises exclusively of a residential district. Each parcel of land possesses distinct characteristics, commanding varying prices, and is epitomized through an NFT. Real estate transactions, which typically involve intricate bureaucratic processes, can be streamlined by integrating pertinent metadata into individualized non-fungible tokens.

Dentraland has successfully incorporated this concept, where it operates as a virtual reality platform built on the Ethereum blockchain. As Non-Fungible Tokens (NFTs) grow in complexity and are integrated into the financial framework, there is potential for the application of tokenized parcels of land, which vary in value and location, within the tangible realm.

INVESTMENT JARGON — EXPLAINED

I believe that the creation of specialized terminology is a result of its efficiency in facilitating communication among individuals.

(Mathematician John Maynard Smith)

Bears

Bears are individuals who express the perspective that the markets are experiencing a decline in value. A bear market can be defined, therefore, as a period during which prices are experiencing a decline.

Blue chip stock

A blue chip stock can be characterized as a large, established corporation that enjoys a strong standing in the market. Google, Coca Cola, and Apple exemplify blue chip stocks.

The advantage of investing in blue chip stocks is that they are unlikely to go bust or suddenly drop in value — but that does not mean they cannot. Enron and Volkswagen were considered to be reputable stocks prior to their share prices being severely affected by scandals.

One drawback associated with blue chip stocks is their limited potential for significant price appreciation. However, it is possible for them to gradually increase over a period of time.

Bulls

Bulls are individuals who express the belief that the financial markets are poised for an upward trajectory. A "bull" market is characterized by a continuous increase in prices.

CFDs

Contracts For Difference. Contract for Differences (CFDs) provide the opportunity to gain exposure to assets without assuming actual ownership of the underlying asset. By utilizing a CFD, one has the ability to invest in commodities such as oil, for instance, without the need to possess physical barrels of oil. CFDs provide opportunities for leveraged trading, which may lead to adverse consequences. Contract for Difference (CFD) trading is presently prohibited within the United States.

Double bottom, double top

Technical charting terminology includes the usage of 'double bottom' and 'double top'.

A "double bottom" refers to a situation where the price of a stock reaches a new low, experiences a slight increase, and then subsequently returns to the same low point. The price bottoms out. Frequently, the cost will subsequently increase. This phenomenon is attributable to the fact that the price has now reached a level where individuals perceive the stock to possess favorable intrinsic value once more.

A "double top" refers to a situation in which the price of a stock reaches a new peak, experiences a slight decline, and subsequently retests the same peak level. The prices tops out. Frequently, the cost will subsequently decrease. This is due to the fact that the price has reached a level wherein individuals perceive the stock to be excessively valued.

Equity

Stocks and shares.

Fundamentals

If you are making the prudent choice of investing for the long term, 'fundamental factors' will prove to be advantageous.

The term 'fundamentals' pertains to the key financial indicators of a business, such as revenue, earnings before interest, taxes, depreciation, and amortization (EBITDA), and the price-to-earnings (P/E) ratio. If the foundational aspects of a company are strong, it indicates effective management and a high likelihood of generating substantial profits in the future.

GBP, USD, EUR

The following demonstrates the notation for specific significant currencies. GBP is an acronym denoting the currency known as the Great British Pound. The acronym USD represents the currency of the United States, known formally as the United States Dollar. EUR stands for Euro.

Going long/going short

To engage in a long position entails the act of purchasing an asset with the expectation that its value will appreciate, enabling a profitable sale in the future.

Engaging in a short position entails purchasing a stock through a specific arrangement that enables one to generate profit upon depreciation of the asset's value. This is frequently referred to as engaging in "stock shorting". The majority of brokers offer this service for stocks. It signifies that one has the capability of generating profits even amidst a decline in market valuations.

Developing A Financial Plan For Real Estate Investment

Annually, there is a growing trend of individuals engaging in real estate investment and utilizing rental properties as a means to expand the diversity of their financial holdings, while simultaneously ensuring a steady stream of income for the future.

Primarily, what are the factors that have precipitated a rise in the quantity of individuals engaging in real estate investment?

Investors have a desire to broaden the range of their holdings.

Individuals express dissatisfaction with the performance of their savings and investments.

The decline in interest rates corresponding to housing values has lead numerous individuals to reassess the feasibility of investing in rental property. Individuals are disengaging from the bond market as a consequence of persistently low interest rates over an extended period.

So, how does this analysis inform your estimation of the necessary monetary resources to prevent overexposure in your investment portfolio? You have the option to utilize two separate approaches in order to ensure that you are making a sound and reliable investment in rental properties.

Rate of Cap

The initial equation is commonly known as the cap rate formula. This formula will calculate the return on investment in the event of a cash purchase of a property. One must divide their net income by the cost of the asset.

As an example,

The monthly rental cost of the property amounts to $1,500, while the total purchase price of the house equates to $200,000.

The estimated monthly expenditures will amount to approximately $500, exclusive of mortgage payments, escrow taxes, and insurance. The monthly net income of this property amounts to $1,000, which equates to an annual sum of approximately $12,000.

Consequently, the capitalization rate equates to $12,000 per $200,000, approximately amounting to 6%.

Can one consider a six percent return on investment as a respectable rate of return?

It ultimately rests within your discretion to determine whether you can reconcile with that. If the locality is reputable, appealing to residents, and attracts tenants of high caliber, the 6% return would be deemed exceptional.

Nevertheless, in the event that the locality exhibits dubious characteristics and carries a significant element of risk, the six percent may fail to justify your investment of time.

Ultimately, the onus lies upon you to thoroughly evaluate the risks associated with potential hazards and assess the level of difficulty in securing tenants for the property, as these factors will determine if the return on investment meets your expectations.

Capital Investment

Investment is a strategic choice that entails the expectation of facilitating the enlargement of financial resources. The excess can be allocated towards a multitude of objectives, including rectifying salary disparities, allocating funds towards retirement savings, or fulfilling specific stipulated obligations, such as reimbursing loans, covering educational expenses, or procuring additional assets.

Having a clear comprehension of the concept of speculation is imperative, as it can sometimes pose challenges in determining the suitable instruments to achieve your financial objectives. Gaining insights into the consequences of speculation on your personal finances can empower you to make optimal choices.

An investment has the potential to generate two streams of profitable returns. Firstly, if you allocate resources towards an asset with resale value, it is possible to receive compensation in the form of a return. Furthermore, by investing in a profit-yielding scheme, your remuneration will be received through the accrual of financial returns.

From a perspective of financial conduct, the term "investment of money" can be elucidated as the act of allocating surplus funds towards assets or commodities that appreciate in value, surpassing their intrinsic worth, or towards those that facilitate the establishment of a self-sustaining income stream.

Trade Traded Funds

Exchange traded funds (ETFs) blend elements of mutual funds and conventional stocks. Similar to a collective resource, an exchange-traded fund (ETF) is a consolidated investment vehicle that provides an investor with a stake in a professionally managed, diversified portfolio of investments. Regardless, in contrast to typical assets, shares of ETFs are traded on stock exchanges like stocks and can be bought and sold at varying prices throughout the trading day.

Are All ETFs Alike?

"Negative. Exchange-traded funds have the potential to undergo shifts in multiple manners:

Administrative design

The majority of exchange-traded funds (ETFs) are registered with the Securities and Exchange Commission (SEC) as investment companies according to the provisions of the Investment Company Act of 1940, and the shares they offer to the public are duly registered under the

Securities Act of 1933. Several exchange-traded funds (ETFs) that invest in commodities, currencies, or derivative instruments based on goods or currencies are not categorized as registered investment companies, despite the fact that their publicly traded shares are registered under the Securities Act.

The board style

There exist a multitude of Exchange-Traded Funds (ETFs) that possess the purpose of passively tracking a designated market index, resembling mutual funds that are tied to a particular index. These exchange-traded funds aim to achieve the identical performance as the benchmark they replicate, through investments in all or a representative sample of the constituent stocks comprising the index. Recently, proficiently managed exchange-traded funds have emerged as an additional alternative for investors. The director responsible for managing a well-controlled ETF engages in stock trading based on an investment strategy, as opposed to adhering to a predetermined list.

Speculation objective

The choice of speculative destinations varies depending on the specific Exchange-Traded Fund (ETF) and its management style. The objective of passively monitoring ETFs is to replicate the performance of the index that the ETF is designed to track. On the contrary, consultants who proficiently manage ETFs contribute to attaining a precise investment objective by making investment decisions autonomously. Certain ETFs that have been overlooked or not widely recognized aim to generate a return that is either higher or lower in value compared to the performance of a specific stock index. These are commonly referred to as used or inverse ETFs. The investment objective of an ETF is stated in its prospectus.

Files followed

Exchange-traded funds (ETFs) accurately replicate a vast array of market indices. Certain records exhibit remarkable breadth in the market, such as comprehensive stock or bond market files. Various exchange-traded funds

(ETFs) follow indices that encompass smaller components, such as medium-sized and small-scale enterprises, exclusively corporate securities, or solely multinational corporations. Several EFTs exhibit remarkably close tracking, and in certain instances, they correspond to exceptionally recent data that is likely to be somewhat convoluted or where limited information is available.

Fundamentals of Exchange-Traded Funds

Unlike traditional assets, ETFs do not directly issue or redeem shares to individual retail investors. In order to render share trading on a stock exchange viable for investors, ETFs adhere to a distinctive structure. An

Exchange-Traded Fund (ETF) enters into agreements with financial institutions (typically large broker dealers) to serve as Authorized Participants (APs). APS engages in the direct acquisition and redemption of shares through the purchase of Creation Units, which consist of sizable blocks of shares within the ETF. Typically, APS engages in the sale of some or all of their ETF shares through a transaction. This enables investors to trade ETF shares in a manner akin to the shares of any publicly traded company.

Chapter Four: Strategic Allocation of Resources to Cryptocurrencies

It appears that digital currencies have gained significant popularity in contemporary times. Since the notable surge of Bitcoin to $20,000 per coin in 2017, the ordinary investor expeditiously apprehended the potential positive aspects of cryptocurrencies. Nonetheless, Bitcoin serves as a cautionary example for all investors. In the future, academic institutions specialized in business education may employ Bitcoin as an instructional tool to impart valuable lessons regarding the perils associated with succumbing to the allure of speculative investments.

When Bitcoin was initially introduced in 2009, there was a lack of comprehensive comprehension regarding its essence and functionality. Consequently, it received little to no attention from anyone. During the initial stages of Bitcoin's existence, its market value was approximately $2 per coin. Indeed, the originators of Bitcoin even presented a portion of them to acquaintances and associates as a symbol of their gratitude for their assistance.

Over a period of time, investors came to recognize the immense potential of Bitcoin as a transformative force in the global economy. Undoubtedly, Bitcoin possessed the capacity to act as the transformative catalyst that would pave the way for a completely digitized economic era.

This phenomenon generated substantial fervor and hullabaloo regarding Bitcoin, leading to a significant increase in its market value. Having started at a modest $2 per coin, its value gradually increased to approximately $1,000 before experiencing an exponential surge towards astronomical heights. It ultimately attained a value of $20,000 by late 2017. Subsequently, the price experienced a significant decline, ultimately reaching approximately $5,000. Over the course of time, the evaluation has remained within the range of $5,000 to $10,000.

Now, the reason why Bitcoin is a cautionary tale lies in the fact that investors piled on as they saw the hype. It appeared that there was a widespread interest in being involved in the endeavor. Their objective was to enter the market at any given price level with the expectation of capitalizing on subsequent price increases. Nevertheless, investors swiftly discovered that this assumption was unfounded. In each wave of enthusiasm, there reaches a juncture where investors exhaust their resources. There comes a juncture wherein purchasers ultimately exhaust their supply. This phenomenon can arise due to either an exorbitant price or the financial constraints faced by investors. Upon reaching that juncture, individuals with ownership positions initiate the process of selling their assets, only to discover a lack of interested buyers. Rapidly, investors commence to experience a sense of urgency and engage in selling their holdings at any available price. The price undergoes a sudden decline. In light of their intense desperation, holders demonstrate a willingness to accept any price. There exist certain investors who hold the belief that they are acquiring a favorable deal. However, they are merely acquiring an asset that is losing value. Once the chaos subsides, a significant number of investors find themselves completely depleted.

This instance serves to exemplify the formation of "bubbles." A bubble occurs when the valuation of an asset is artificially inflated, meaning that its price does not accurately reflect its genuine and inherent worth. Indeed, the price valuation emanates from the investors' discernment of its inherent worth. Once the bubble inevitably collapses, a cohort of investors is left solely with shattered aspirations.

Arguably, one of the most detrimental aspects of the Bitcoin bubble was the unfortunate reality that ordinary individuals liquidated their assets or incurred debt in order to fund their investment in Bitcoin. In the end, they were left with an unfavorable experience. Hence, it is crucial to bear in mind the Bitcoin bubble phenomenon when examining a prospective market opportunity.